AMAZING ORIGAMI

Desert Origami

Joe Fullman

Gareth Stevens
PUBLISHING

Please visit our website, www.garethstevens.com.
For a free color catalog of all our high-quality books,
call toll free 1-800-542-2595 or fax 1-877-542-2596.

Cataloging-in-Publication Data

Names: Fullman, Joe.
Title: Desert origami / Joe Fullman.
Description: New York : Gareth Stevens, 2017. | Series: Amazing origami | Includes index.
Identifiers: ISBN 9781482459241 (pbk.) | ISBN 9781482459265 (library bound) | ISBN 9781482459258 (6 pack)
Subjects: LCSH: Origami--Juvenile literature. | Desert animals in art--Juvenile literature. | Animals in art--Juvenile literature.
Classification: LCC TT872.5 F85 2017 | DDC 736.982--dc23

First Edition

Published in 2017 by
Gareth Stevens Publishing
111 East 14th Street, Suite 349
New York, NY 10003

Models and photography: Belinda Webster and Michael Wiles
Text: Joe Fullman
Design: Tokiko Morishima
Editor: Frances Evans

Printed in China

CPSIA compliance information: Batch CW17GS:
For further information contact Gareth Stevens, New York, New York at 1-800-542-2595.

Contents

Basic Folds

Origami has been popular in Japan for hundreds of years and is now loved all around the world. You can make great models with just one sheet of paper... and this book shows you how!

Origami paper is thin but strong, so that it can be folded many times. It is usually colored on one side. You can use ordinary scrap paper, but make sure it's not too thick.

Origami models often share the same folds and basic designs. This introduction explains some of the folds that you will need for the projects in this book. When making the models, follow the key below to find out what the lines and arrows mean. And always crease well! Ask an adult to help you with any project that needs scissors.

KEY

valley fold	- - - - - - -	step fold (mountain and valley fold next to each other)
mountain fold	....	direction to move paper
		push

Cut here

turn paper over

rotate by x degrees

MOUNTAIN FOLD

To make a mountain fold, fold the paper so that the crease is pointing up towards you, like a mountain.

VALLEY FOLD

To make a valley fold, fold the paper the other way, so that the crease is pointing away from you, like a valley.

STEP FOLD

A step fold is used to make a step or zigzag in the paper. We'll use it to make ears, tails, and other animal features. Practice with a full sheet of paper first.

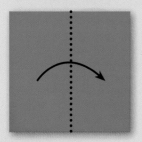

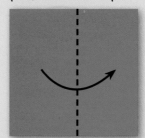

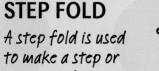

(1) Valley fold the paper in half. Then make a mountain fold directly above the valley fold.

(2) Push the mountain fold over the valley fold and press down flat.

(3) You now have a step fold. You can also make it in reverse, with the mountain fold first.

INSIDE REVERSE FOLD

An inside reverse fold is useful if you want to make a nose or a tail, or if you want to flatten off the shape of another part of an origami model.

① Practice by first folding a piece of paper diagonally in half. Make a valley fold on one point and crease.

② It's important to make sure that the paper is creased well. Run your finger over the crease two or three times.

③ Unfold and open up the corner slightly. Refold the crease you just made into a mountain fold.

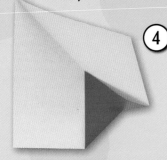

④ Open up the paper a little more and then tuck the tip of the point inside. Close the paper. This is the view from the underside of the paper.

⑤ Flatten the paper. You now have an inside reverse fold.

OUTSIDE REVERSE FOLD

An outside reverse fold is useful if you want to make a head, beak or foot, or another part of your model that sticks out.

① Practice by first folding a piece of paper diagonally in half. Make a valley fold on one point and crease.

② It's important to make sure that the paper is creased well. Run your finger over the crease two or three times.

③ Unfold and open up the corner slightly. Refold the crease you just made into a valley fold.

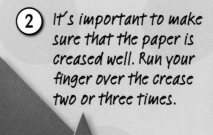

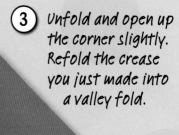

④ Open up the paper a little more and start to turn the corner inside out. Then close the paper when the fold begins to turn.

⑤ You now have an outside reverse fold. You can either flatten the paper or leave it rounded out.

Burrowing Owl

These cute feathered critters live in burrows beneath the hot desert sand. Here's how to fold your own origami version.

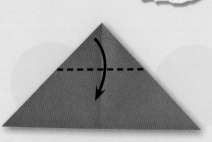

① Place your paper white side up with a corner facing you. Valley fold it in half from left to right, then unfold.

② Fold the paper in half from bottom to top.

③ Fold the top point of the top layer down, as shown.

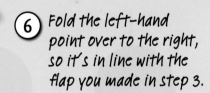

④ Make a valley fold in the top layer, as shown.

⑤ Fold the top point down and slightly over the flap you made in step 4.

⑥ Fold the left-hand point over to the right, so it's in line with the flap you made in step 3.

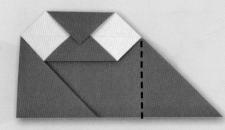

Unfold   Unfold

⑦ Repeat step 6 on the right-hand side. The new flap will go slightly over the one you made in step 6.

⑧ Unfold the flaps you made in steps 6 and 7.

9 Turn the paper over from left to right.

10 Fold the left and right points down, as shown, using the fold marks you made in steps 6 and 7 as a guide.

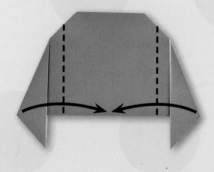

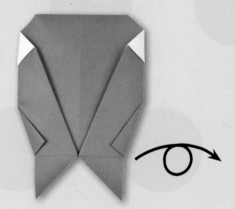

11 Fold the new left and right points over to the central line, as shown.

12 Fold the bottom corners of the new left and right points in, as shown.

13 Your paper should look like this. Turn it over from left to right.

Did You Know?

Despite their name, burrowing owls don't actually dig their own burrows. Instead they move into holes that have been left behind by other desert creatures, such as ground squirrels and prairie dogs.

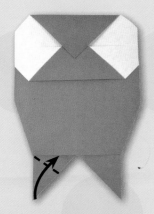

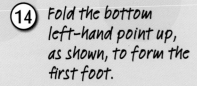

(14) Fold the bottom left-hand point up, as shown, to form the first foot.

(15) Repeat step 14 on the right-hand side.

(16) Fold over the left-hand foot, as shown.

(17) Repeat step 16 on the right-hand side.

(18) Your little desert owl is ready to scurry off across the sand.

Snake

Snakes are cold-blooded, so they warm themselves up by lying in the sun. Try not to get too hot and squirmy when folding yours!

① Place your paper like this, with the white side up and a corner facing you. Make a valley fold from left to right, then unfold.

② Fold the left corner to the central crease.

③ Fold the right corner to the central crease.

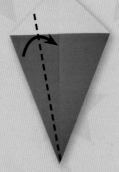

④ Again, fold the left corner to the middle.

⑤ Repeat step 4 on the right-hand side.

⑥ Make a valley fold, as shown, on the top left-hand side of the paper. It should also meet the central line.

⑦ Repeat step 6 on the right-hand side.

⑧ Your paper should look like this. Turn it over from left to right, and then rotate it 90° to the left.

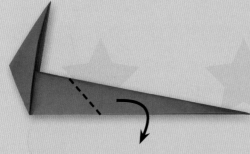

(9) Mountain fold the paper in half from top to bottom. Rotate it to the right so the straight, long edge is facing you.

(10) Make a valley fold, like this. Fold it the other way to make a mountain fold. Then turn it into an outside reverse fold (see page 5).

(11) Make a valley fold slightly farther down the paper. Fold it the other way, so it's also a mountain fold, then fold it in on itself.

(12) Your paper should be loose, rather than flat, like this. Repeat step 11 four more times further along the paper, in the positions marked.

Did You Know?

Many desert snakes are sidewinders, which means they move sideways rather than forwards. This allows them to lift parts of their body off of the sand as they move, stopping them from becoming too hot.

13 Your paper should look like this. Make a valley fold at the left-hand end, as shown.

14 Fold it back the other way so it's also a mountain fold. Then fold it over itself to form an outside reverse fold.

Tuck

15 Fold it back the other way so it's also a mountain fold. Then tuck it in to form an inside reverse fold (see page 5).

16 Make a small valley fold at the left-hand end, as shown.

17 Add some eyes and your snake is ready to slither – forwards or sideways, it's up to you.

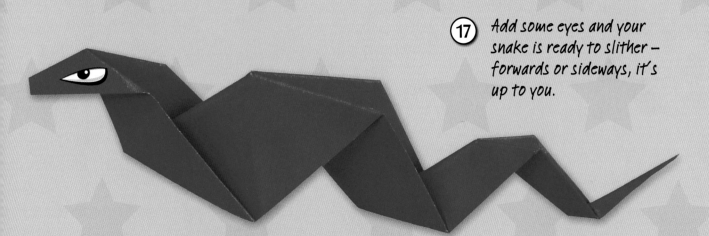

Tortoise

Desert tortoises have brown-colored shells which camouflage them against their sandy surroundings. They also hardly ever drink. Instead they get their water from the plants they eat.

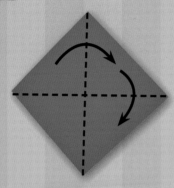

1 Place your paper white side down with a corner facing you. Valley fold it in half from top to bottom, and unfold. Then valley fold it in half from left to right, and unfold.

2 Turn the paper over, so that the white side is now facing up. Diagonally valley fold it one way, and unfold. Then diagonally valley fold it the other way, and unfold.

Push

Push

3 Start pushing the two outer corners in towards each other.

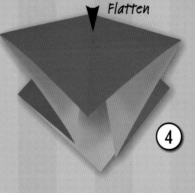

Flatten

4 As you push, the paper should start folding up into a small square like this. Flatten it down.

5 Fold the left-hand point of the top layer over to the central crease.

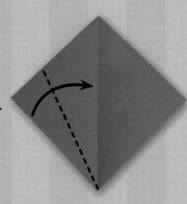

6 Fold the right-hand point of the top layer over to the central crease.

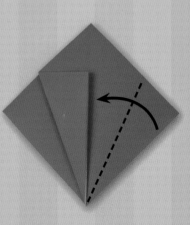

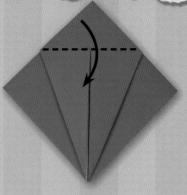

⑦ Fold the top point down, as shown.

⑧ Unfold the folds you made in steps 5, 6, and 7.

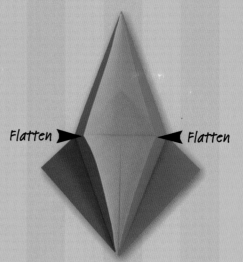

Flatten ▶◀   ▶◀ Flatten

⑨ Lift up the bottom point of the top layer up to the top.

⑩ Your paper should form a shape a bit like a bird's mouth. Flatten the sides down.

Did You Know?

Tortoises use their powerful front claws to dig burrows in the desert sand. These can be up to 5 feet (1.5 m) deep, allowing the tortoises to rest far away from the heat of the sun.

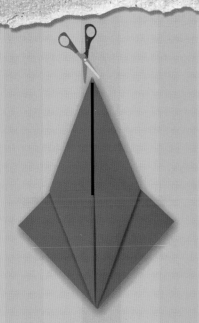

11 Using scissors, make a cut from the top point to the central crease. Don't cut across the triangle at the back.

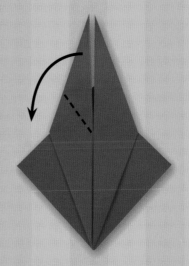

12 Fold the top left point over to the left.

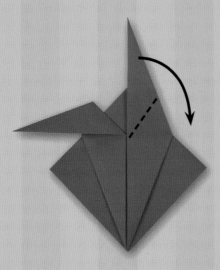

13 Fold the top right point over to the right.

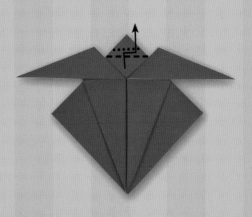

14 Make a step fold at the top, as shown.

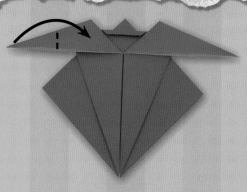

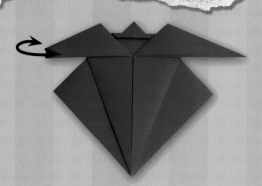

(15) Your paper should look like this. Fold the top left-hand point to the right.

(16) Fold it the other way, so it's also a mountain fold.

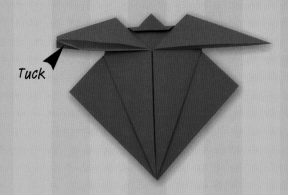

Tuck

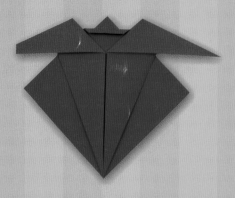

(17) Open up the fold and tuck it in to form an inside reverse fold (see page 5).

(18) Your paper should look like this. Repeat steps 15 to 17 on the right-hand side.

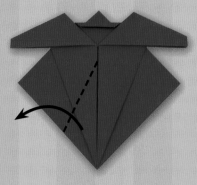

(19) Fold the bottom left point across to the left, as shown.

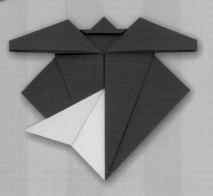

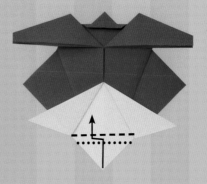

20 Your paper should look like this. Repeat step 19 on the other side.

21 Make a step fold at the bottom, as shown.

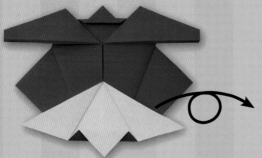

22 Your paper should look like this. Turn it over from left to right.

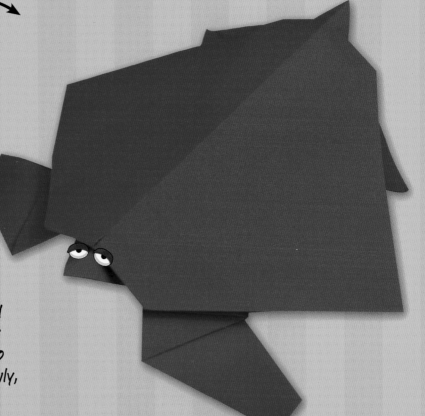

23 Slightly fold the shell and point the legs down. Your tortoise should be able to stand and walk (very slowly, of course).

Camel

The camel is perhaps the most famous and recognizable desert animal of all. Follow these instructions to make your own one-humped version, also known as a dromedary.

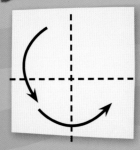

1. Place your paper white side up with a straight edge facing you. Valley fold it in half from top to bottom, and unfold. Then valley fold it in half from left to right, and unfold.

2. Turn the paper over, so that the white side is now facing down. Diagonally valley fold it one way and unfold. Then diagonally valley fold it the other way and unfold.

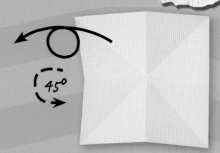

3. Turn the paper over again, so the white side is facing up. Rotate it 45° so a corner is facing you.

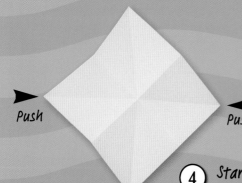

Push   Push

4. Start pushing the two outer corners in towards each other.

Flatten

5. As you push, the paper should start folding up into a small square like this. Flatten it down.

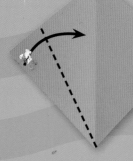

6. Fold the left-hand point of the top layer over to the central crease.

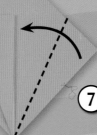

7. Fold the right-hand point of the top layer over to the central crease.

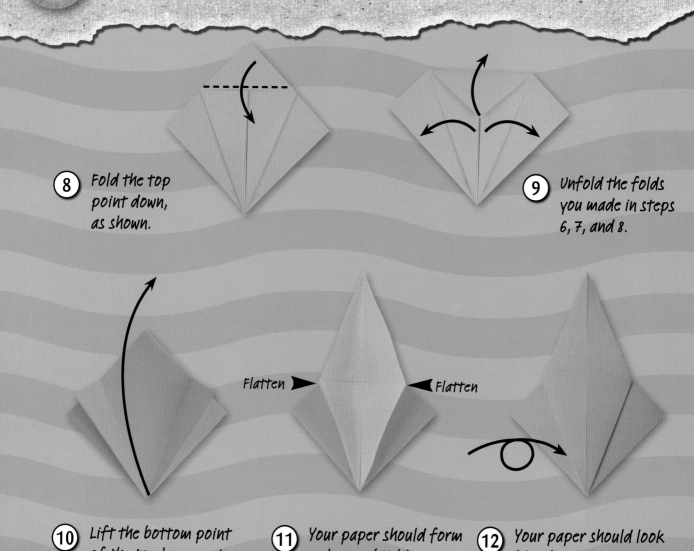

8 Fold the top point down, as shown.

9 Unfold the folds you made in steps 6, 7, and 8.

Flatten ▶ ◀ Flatten

10 Lift the bottom point of the top layer up to the top.

11 Your paper should form a shape a bit like a bird's mouth. Flatten the sides down.

12 Your paper should look like this. Turn it over from left to right.

13 Now, repeat steps 6 to 11 on this side of the model.

14 Your paper should now look like this. Fold the left-hand point of the top layer over to the central crease.

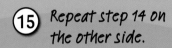

15 Repeat step 14 on the other side.

16 Your paper should look like this. Turn it over from left to right.

17 Fold the left-hand point over to the central crease.

18 Fold the right-hand point over to the central crease.

19 Valley fold the bottom left point up and to the left, as shown.

Did You Know?

A camel's hump is made of fat, not water as lots of people think – although camels can go for a very long time without drinking.

20 Fold it the other way so it's also a mountain fold.

21 Open up the fold and tuck it in to form an inside reverse fold (see page 5).

Tuck

22 Your paper should look like this. Repeat steps 19 to 21 on the other side.

23 Valley fold the right-hand point down, and then back the other way so it's also a mountain fold.

Tuck

24 Open up the fold and tuck it in to form an inside reverse fold.

25 Valley fold down the top point of the top layer to form the first front leg.

26 Your paper should look this. Mountain fold the remaining top point down to form the other front leg and reveal the hump.

27 Valley fold the top left point over to the left, as shown.

28 Fold it the other way, so it's also a mountain fold, then tuck it inside to form an inside reverse fold.

29 Make a valley fold. Fold it the other way, so it's also a mountain fold. Then tuck it inside to form an inside reverse fold.

30 Mountain fold the top layer of the right corner, and tuck the flap inside the paper.

32 Pull the front legs out slightly, and your camel should be able to stand up.

31 Your paper should look like this. Repeat step 30 on the other side.

Vulture

These large meat-eating birds live in large groups called committees. Vultures have excellent senses of sight and smell, which help them find food.

1 Place your paper white side up with a straight edge facing you. Valley fold in half from top to bottom, and unfold. Then valley fold in half from left to right, and unfold.

2 Turn the paper over, so that the white side is now facing down. Diagonally valley fold it one way and unfold. Then diagonally valley fold it the other way and unfold.

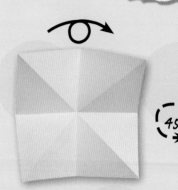

3 Turn the paper over again, so the white side is facing up. Rotate it 45° so a corner is facing you.

Push   Push

4 Start pushing the two outer corners in towards each other.

Flatten

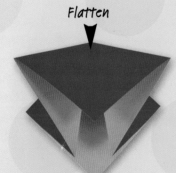

5 As you push, the paper should start folding up into a small square like this. Flatten it down.

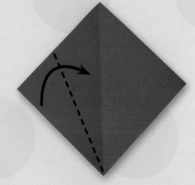

6 Fold the left-hand point of the top layer over to the central crease.

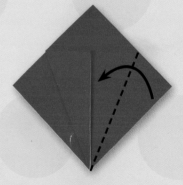

7 Fold the right-hand point of the top layer over to the central crease.

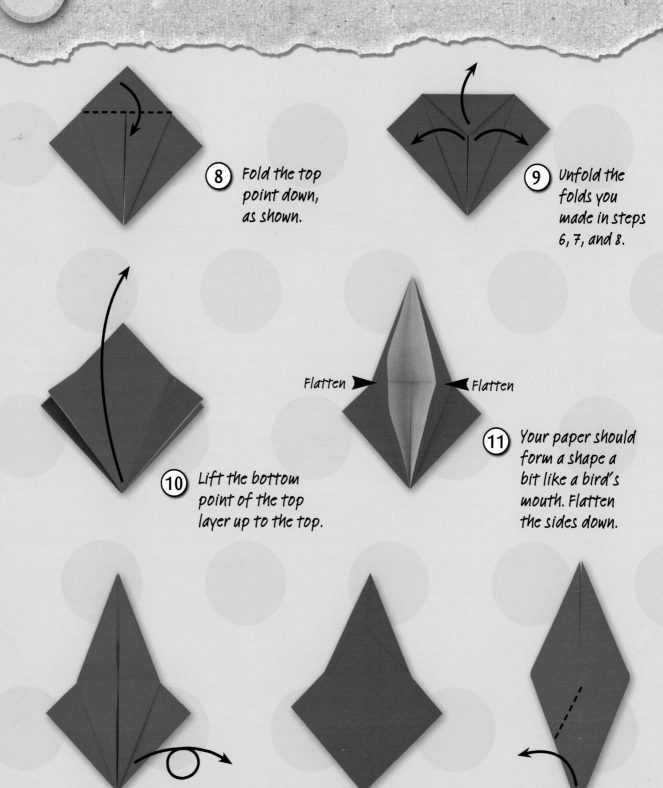

8 Fold the top point down, as shown.

9 Unfold the folds you made in steps 6, 7, and 8.

10 Lift the bottom point of the top layer up to the top.

Flatten ◄   ►Flatten

11 Your paper should form a shape a bit like a bird's mouth. Flatten the sides down.

12 Your paper should look like this. Turn it over from left to right.

13 Now, repeat steps 6 to 11 on this side.

14 Fold the bottom left point over to the left, as shown.

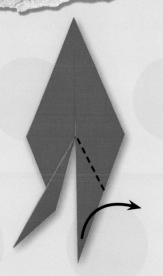

Turn over

15 Repeat step 14 on the right-hand side.

16 Turn the fold you made in step 14 over on itself to form an outside reverse fold (see page 5).

17 Your paper should look like this. Repeat step 16 on the right-hand side.

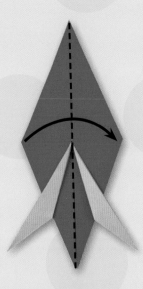

18 Bring the top point of the back layer down to the bottom.

19 Valley fold your paper in half from left to right.

20 Rotate your paper slightly to the right.

21 Fold the bottom point over to the right.

22 Now fold the tip of that point down to form the first foot.

23 Your paper should look like this. Repeat steps 21 and 22 on the other side to form the second foot.

24 Mountain fold the top point over and to the right, as shown.

25 Make another mountain fold in the opposite direction slightly farther to the right.

26 Your paper should look like this. Turn the folds you made in steps 24 and 25 into two inside reverse folds, one inside the other (see page 5).

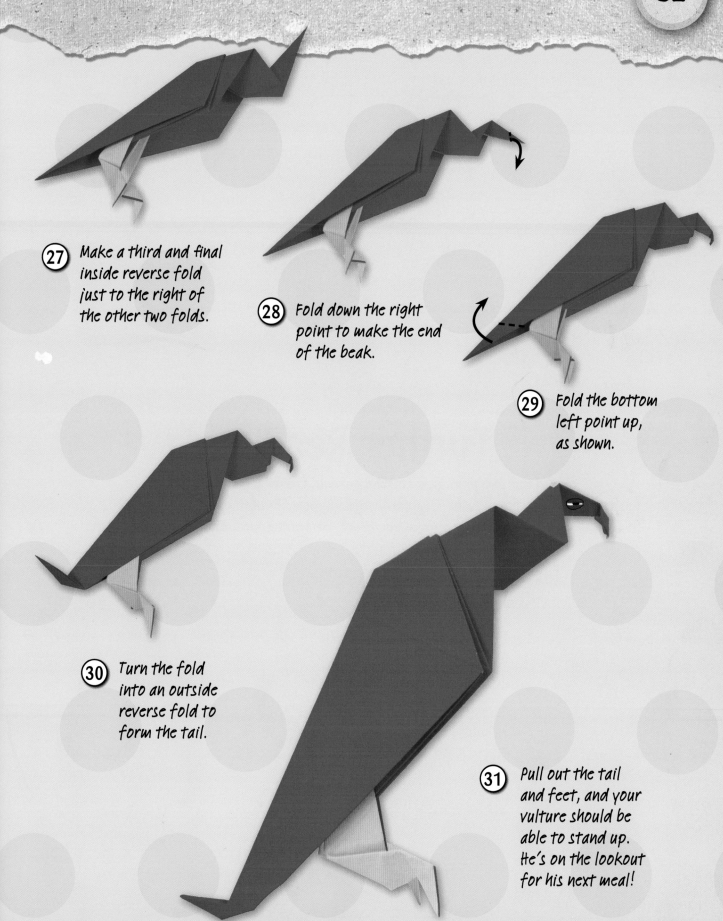

27 Make a third and final inside reverse fold just to the right of the other two folds.

28 Fold down the right point to make the end of the beak.

29 Fold the bottom left point up, as shown.

30 Turn the fold into an outside reverse fold to form the tail.

31 Pull out the tail and feet, and your vulture should be able to stand up. He's on the lookout for his next meal!

Glossary

burrow A small tunnel dug by an animal, often as a place for it to live. Burrowing is the act of digging.

camouflage Colors, markings or patterns on an animal that help it to blend into the background.

crease A line in a piece of paper made by folding.

inside reverse fold An origami step where the paper is folded in on itself creating a flattened shape.

mountain fold An origami step where a piece of paper is folded so that the crease is pointing upwards, like a mountain.

outside reverse fold An origami step where the paper is folded back over itself.

predator An animal that hunts and eats other animals for food.

rotate To move something in a circle around its central point.

step fold A mountain fold and valley fold next to each other.

valley fold An origami step where a piece of paper is folded so that the crease is pointing downwards, like a valley.

Further Reading

Montroll, John. *Easy Origami Animals*. Dover Children's, 2015.

Percy, Tasha. *Origami Animals*. Templar Publishing, 2016.

Robinson, Nick. *The Awesome Origami Pack*. Barron's Educational Series, Inc., 2014.

Index